BEDROOMS

Design
Is in the
Details

Brad Mee

Sterling Publishing Co., Inc. New York
A Sterling/Chapelle Book

Chapelle, Ltd.:
Jo Packham
Sara Toliver
Cindy Stoeckl

Editor: Karla Haberstich
Copy Editor: Marilyn Goff
Cover: Photography: Dino Tonn
    Interior Design: David Michael Miller

If you have any questions or comments, please contact:
Chapelle, Ltd., Inc., P.O. Box 9252, Ogden, UT 84409
    (801) 621-2777 • (801) 621-2788 Fax
    e-mail: chapelle@chapelleltd.com
    web site: www.chapelleltd.com

Library of Congress Cataloging-in-Publication Data
Mee, Brad
        Bedrooms : design is in the details / Brad Mee.
            p.   cm.
        "A Sterling/Chapelle book."
        Includes index.
        ISBN 1-4027-0669-3
        1. Bedrooms. 2. Interior decoration. I. Title.
    NK2117.B4M44   2003
    747.7'7--dc21
                                            2003008826

10 9 8 7 6 5 4 3 2 1

Published in paperback in 2006 by Sterling Publishing Co., Inc.
387 Park Avenue South, New York, NY 10016
© 2003 by Brad Mee
Distributed in Canada by Sterling Publishing,
c/o Canadian Manda Group, 165 Dufferin Street,
Toronto, Ontario, Canada M6K 3H6
Distributed in the United Kingdom by GMC Distribution Services,
Castle Place, 166 High Street, Lewes, East Sussex, England BN7 1XU
Distributed in Australia by Capricorn Link (Australia) Pty. Ltd.
P.O. Box 704, Windsor, NSW 2756, Australia
Printed and Bound in China
All Rights Reserved

Sterling ISBN-13: 978-1-4027-0669-1 Hardcover
            ISBN-10: 1-4027-0669-3

            ISBN-13: 978-1-4027-3454-0 Paperback
            ISBN-10: 1-4027-3454-9

For information about custom editions, special sales, premium and
corporate purchases, please contact Sterling Special Sales
Department at 800-805-5489 or specialsales@sterlingpub.com.

CONTENTS

INTRODUCTION

Remember when being sent to your bedroom was considered a form of punishment? Today, this type of domestic discipline hardly works given the state of this stylish space. For most of us, it is now considered a treat to spend time in the bedroom. It is being used for more than just sleeping. Reading, relaxing, exercising, and simply escaping the outside world top the list of activities the room accommodates. Whatever functions it performs, as a retreat, the bedroom is unbeatable. As a room deserving personal detail and design, it is unmatched.

At one time, the bedroom was thought of as little more than a place to sleep. Any decorative and design efforts were modest and mostly saved for the home's more public spaces like the living, dining, and family rooms. Because the bedroom is private, somewhat removed from the rest of the home, and rarely shared with "outsiders," its aesthetic potential was often ignored and overlooked. It simply was not deemed important. Things have certainly changed. Now, for these very same reasons—privacy, seclusion, personal space—the room is lavished with detail that enhances our desire to retreat, rest, and revitalize within its walls. We look at the bedroom as a private sanctuary and, as a result, are donning it with treatments and details that are uniquely personal and very indulgent.

For as many individuals as there are in the world, there are an equal number of ways to decorate the bedroom. Some prefer a romantic approach that indulges the room with luxury and richness. Others want a clean, tailored look that frees them from the excess and confusion of day-to-day living. Still others dream of a fantasy space that is filled with exotic elements which speak of faraway places and fascinating scenes. Whatever its theme or direction, it is the function of detail to bring the desired style to life. Through color, texture, scale, and imaginative treatments, detail can turn the bedroom and all of its contents into a form of personal expression. Detail allows you to put your unique signature of style on your private suite.

STYLE

Do you dream of the perfect bedroom, . . . one that embraces you in rich character and seduces you with stunning style? Your dreamy domain need not exist only in your sleep. By using unique and personal detail, it can be brought to life and enjoyed during your waking hours as well. First, you must determine your ideal bedroom; define its style. Comfort is the prevailing language of all well-designed bedrooms. How it is translated and interpreted depends upon the individual. To some, soothing, soft, and serene is comforting. To others, clean-lined clarity is the most relaxing; while still others find plush, sumptuous opulence the most blissful. For each individual, there is a unique perfect bedroom. To create yours, simply "follow your dreams" and use detail to bring it to life.

The sophisticated bedroom, at its best, is like a dry martini. Clean, cool, and oh-so-nice to come home to after a hard day's work. It welcomes its owners with an understated sense of elegance—a simple yet rich ambience. The style is neither coldly modern nor oppressively traditional. It is smooth, timeless, and unpretentious. Muted tones unify the elements of the room—surfaces, furnishings, accents. Soft natural shades of taupe, ivory, gray, and brown most successfully accomplish this. Black may underscore the room's color story while a spot of color or sheen may offer a shot of

SOPHISTICATED

tempered glamour. A juxtaposition of materials flavors the room with a mix of rough and refined; linen plays against polished wood, glass pairs with chiseled stone, and velvet teams with marble. Texture, rather than pattern, is used to bring rhythm and motion to the space. Accessories are minimal; lighting is subdued. The lines of the furnishings may be either round or square as long as they are clean and uncluttered. The beauty of the sophisticated bedroom is its ability to relax with its harmonious simplicity, yet stimulate with its intriguing use of materials and design.

OPPOSITE
Cool shades of platinum and gray give this master suite a refined and sophisticated feel. The absence of skirts on the armless chairs and sofa make the room seem more spacious and streamlined. While the upholstered pieces visually open the area, heavy velvet drapes counterbalance this effect and help give a cozy feel.

UPPER LEFT
Fitted bedding eliminates the fussiness of elaborate bedding ensembles and brings an air of sophistication to this bedroom. The square quilted pattern of the bedspread creates a tailored look that is repeated in the linear designs of the floating nightstand, square pillows, and simple headboard.

LOWER LEFT
Black is the perfect accent color for the sophisticated bedroom. When played against natural shades of tan and taupe, it adds a sense of definition and drama to the room.

Sit back, close your eyes and imagine the most comforting bedroom you can. Do you envision piles of fluffy pillows, a lofty down comforter, and streams of natural light warming the room? Maybe you see vintage fabrics immersed in soft colors and patterns, blond wood floors, and white sheer draperies swaying in the breeze. If this is the case, then the relaxed-style bedroom is for you. This room is made for sunny afternoon naps and leisurely weekend mornings spent reading the paper in bed. It is soft, nurturing, and peaceful. Natural materials reign throughout. Wood floors, woven rugs, and tongue-and-groove walls set the stage for soft furnishings and unpretentious accents. The room may lean toward contemporary with mellowed solid colors and simple accessories. On the other hand, it may be traditional and filled with a mixture of

RELAXED

unmatched linens, a painted iron-frame bed, and distressed period furniture. The relaxed bedroom is perfectly suited for a beachfront cottage, a cabin in the woods, or a parkside bungalow with windows open to the night skies. Wherever it calls home, it brings deep-seated comfort and unmistakable charm to those who wrap themselves in its embrace.

Fashions fade; style is eternal.

Yves Saint Laurent

ABOVE AND OPPOSITE UPPER RIGHT
A harmonious play of natural light and muted shades of
buttermilk and yellow brings a warm serene feel to this
space. Furnishings are kept subtle and soft to allow the
simplicity of the space to shine through.

The relaxed bedroom is a celebration of simple and honest detail. Comfort is the guide as every element of the room is chosen for its ability to bring visual and emotional serenity to the space. All of the senses are nurtured with the freshness and calmness of the room. The floors are soft underfoot with polished wood, scattered rugs, or natural sisal. The walls, seemingly padded in sun-washed colors, may be covered with painted paneling, floral or striped papers, or satin-finished paint. The bed may be grand and impressive or low and understated. In either case, it is the linens that cover it that set the tone for the room. Quilted cotton, soft linen, and warm woolen blankets are mixed and matched with downy pillows and cushy bolsters. Comforters, coverlets, and spreads are used as the seasons direct. Windows welcome the outdoors in and, when necessary, soft sheers, natural blinds, or painted shutters can provide privacy. Down to the antique glass doorknobs, the accents and accessories are simple and unpretentious. Nothing is staged or orderly; the selection is relaxed and the display spontaneous. Flowers fill pottery vases and natural light is treasured as it fills the room. Softly shaded lamps help illuminate the area with a peaceful glow. There is no fad or fashion to the restful bedroom, only a timelessness that caresses with the ease and blissfulness of its style.

PAGE 19
This large canopy bed is ideally scaled for this relaxed room. It is left undraped to accentuate its carvings and to maintain the open, airy feel of the space.

LEFT
Bold in its shape and design, this lamp is softened by its lack of color and unadorned white shade. It makes a stylish yet quiet addition to a relaxed-style bedroom.

Anything for a quiet life.

Charles Dickens

OPPOSITE
Cool and tranquil, blue and white are classic
color companions in a relaxed bedroom. A
splash of bright sunny yellow or spring green
brings warmth to the space and adds
a touch of cheer.

ABOVE
Like a backlight, a sunny window can softly
accent the visual strength of well-chosen
accessories. This balanced composition of
translucent shaded lamps and distinctive
planters is enhanced by the natural light
that shines from behind.

Soft music, flickering candlelight, and fabrics that tell tales centuries old, . . . these are just a few of the dancers in a well-choreographed rich bedroom. A romantic at heart, this Old World space is a timeless refuge from modern-day living. It looks to the past to enrich the present and freely draws upon the most splendid of periods and faraway lands to create its lavish charm. The inspirations for this richly styled bedroom are plentiful and can reflect Italian, Spanish, or French influences, as well as many others. The style is indulgent, opulent, and timeless. In many richly styled bedrooms, glowing wood and polished stone floors play host to extravagantly patterned rugs. Walls are softly tinted, deeply glazed, or ornately papered. They are deeply finished to draw the room in—to clutch it softly like a velvet glove. Shapely furnishings boast ornate carvings, gentle curves, and distressed unmatched finishes. Selected for their individual charm, the furnishings work together to create the enduring beauty of the space. Copious amounts of fabric—rich velvets, brocades, silks—spill from grand canopies and rods, puddling luxuriously on the floor. The bed is the throne of the room and is dressed accordingly. Its bedding ensemble is exquisitely fabricated and embellished with elaborate trims, tassels, and braids. Cloud-like comforters, plush pillows and the finest linens are teamed. Soft light may fall from an overhead chandelier or from elegant lamps

RICH

that create pools of ambience throughout the room. Accessories embody the charm of the ages and include crystal vases, marble busts, treasured artifacts, and heirloom collectibles. The details of this expressive style are truly personal. They give the bedroom a look that is as timeless as it is beautiful.

The rich bedroom shuns modern-day furnishings and fixtures, turning instead to the ageless appeal of Old World elements. Electronics are stored behind beautifully carved doors of stately armoires, remote controls are placed in leather tabletop boxes, and alarm clocks are cleverly fashioned to replicate antique timepieces. The room contrasts details both rugged and refined. Finishes of wood and metal are often unmatched and distressed to impart age and character to the room. While many pieces flaunt timeworn patinas, others contrast with touches of gold and hand-painted detailing. This mix is important so the space does not appear staged or contrived. Fabrics profusely swathe ornately carved furnishings and bold architecture with billowing softness and jewel-like trims. They should be used liberally, cascading from extravagant canopies, layered on skirted bedside tables, and embellishing beds and upholstered pieces with vintage patterns and sumptuous textures. The lighting is seductive and should be adjustable to set the tone at any given moment. The bedside lamp is just one of many lighting options—shapely sconces, an elegant chandelier, torchères, and hidden uplights are ideal ways to illuminate and enhance the room's ambience. Accessories abound—treasured photos in silver frames, European oil paintings, leather-bound books, and elegant vases filled with flowers that speak the language of romance. Illusions of grandeur lord over the space as excess in detail becomes the hallmark of this richly appointed room.

PAGE 25
Large-scale furnishings, a dramatic use of fabric, and multiple sources of ambient light are used to fill and soften the ample space of this Old World master suite. The robust floral patterns of the exquisite rugs draw the voluminous space inward to make it cozy and intimate.

LEFT
The rich bedroom reflects a life of indulgence and sumptuous comfort. Deep colors and elaborate carvings ensure the passion of this style as they bring opulence to the space.

OPPOSITE
This suite's rich regal tones and a profuse play of pattern on top of pattern create the lavishness and romance necessary for an Old World bedroom. The large-scale treatment that lords over the bed is beautifully balanced by the generously sized, elaborately carved bench at its base.

Whatever the uses of a room, it should be a world unto itself.

Edith Wharton

OPPOSITE
Exquisite fabrics are one key to creating a richly styled bedroom. They instill luxury and refinement to the room while counterbalancing the sometimes aged and distressed qualities of the room's other decorative elements.

ABOVE AND LEFT
Not all rich bedrooms are elegant and refined. Many derive their charm from weighty pieces enriched by texture and tone. In this room, robust, elaborately carved furnishings are at home when paired with fine fabrics, hand-plastered walls, and a palette of glowing golden ocher. The heavy yet heavenly look reflects the ambience of a centuries-old Spanish retreat.

For many, the clean lines and uncluttered simplicity of the modern bedroom create a sanctuary that cannot be beaten. It offers a freedom and escape from the excesses of the outside world. It is peaceful in its purity, refreshing in its refinement. It can run the gamut from minimal and edgy to gentle and warm. In any case, because there is no excess in the modern bedroom, every decorative element must earn its keep. Each is selected for the function it serves and the style it provides. Clutter is not welcome here. Floors set the stage with cool concrete, light-toned polished woods, or structured carpets. Walls become canvases of bold or demure colors and play host to expanses of

MODERN

glass, translucent doors, focused art, and architectural attributes. Niches and insets are good; molding, wainscoting, and cornices are not. The rule is sleek and spare. The bed is often the modern-styled suite's focal point and, therefore, its style is very significant. It can be low slung, emphasizing a horizontal line in the room, or a boxy canopy or four-poster bed that fills the room's space with geometric presence. No draping or layer-upon-layer of fabrics is appropriate, neither are stacks and piles of pillows. Bedding should be tailored and simple, its interest derived from texture and tone. Furniture is selected to heighten the room's style. The importance of its design is only equaled by the function it serves. It must provide comfort to ease the room's guests and ample storage to hide its clutter. Window treatments, when necessary, are minimal and restrained; so are accessories. Bold statements of art, sculpture, and ingenious light fixtures are often the most fitting ways to accent the room while keeping it pristine and clean.

The details of a well-designed modern bedroom play to the nature of the space and take advantage of its architectural attributes. Broad windows are left unobstructed, angled walls exaggerated with color, and niches and insets emphasized with stylistic lighting. Material interest is paramount and the surface and finish of each and every element of the room is utilized as a way to contribute to the room's style. When you create a modern bedroom, think outside of the box. A sleigh bed of stainless steel, a cushioned armchair fashioned from stone, and a screen with panels of etched glass are all examples of serviceable, stylish additions to the room. The trick is to remain focused on the simplicity and clarity of the space while being imaginative in its design and details.

PAGE 31
Double doors bring a sense of drama
to a room's entry and create a sense of
spaciousness and light. In this bedroom,
they work in tandem with an inset
architectural ceiling and hallway
details that frame the room's interior
like a piece of art.

RIGHT
The power of repetition in design should not
be underestimated. In this stunning space, the
rectangular slotted windows of an exterior wall
inspire similar shapes in the carpet, bedding,
architectural insets, and fireplace. Rounded
seating pieces and sculpted orbs wonderfully
soften the hard edges of the room.

Architecture is inhabited sculpture.

Constantin Brancusi

ABOVE
The modern style celebrates bold architectural details.
This bedroom appears to be floating among panes of
floor-to-ceiling glass. To anchor it in place, a weighty
grouping of art is placed above a sizable bed. The
room's carpeting delineates the room from an adjacent
space surfaced with wood flooring, thus further
defining the bedroom area.

BELOW
A continuum of boxy shapes and hard angles establishes the modern style of this bedroom. Minimal accessories, distinctive hardware, and an understated fireplace surround are in keeping with the pristine design of the space.

RIGHT
Loft living lends itself to modern design. This bedroom's built-in cabinetry allows for minimal furnishings, leaving the focus where it should be—on the interesting architectural and surface treatments throughout. Large untreated windows add a light and spacious feeling to the home.

If you dream about exotic and faraway places, why not create a bedroom that takes you there? Your bedroom can be a temporary escape from your daily routine as it transports you to some tropical island or foreign land. All it takes is a venturesome spirit, a discerning eye, and imaginative details. Begin with a theme, then determine your inspiration and set your course. Let this guide you as you select the room's details. First, choose a statement piece—a unique bed, distinctive piece of artwork or sculpture, or perhaps an exotic rug or fabric. As the main focal point, this is the style driver for the space. Enrich the room's surfaces to create the perfect backdrop for this piece.

EXOTIC

For instance, if you dream of creating a tropical bedroom, you may choose a plantation style canopy bed, and then stylize it with bamboo flooring, grass-cloth wall coverings, and a thatched ceiling supporting a large breezy ceiling fan. Use materials and colors indigenous to your dreamy locale—anything from cool seaside hues and bleached driftwood to spicy Mediterranean colors and chiseled stone. Next come the accents and accessories. These are the jewels that complete the look. Potted palms, tribal textiles, animal prints, and one-of-a-kind lamps, . . . it all depends on your determined design direction. Any element of intrigue that exudes the flavor of your dream destination will help shape your exotic bedroom.

As the world has become smaller and the products and designs from around the globe more accessible, creating an exotic bedroom no longer requires a travel agent and ticket abroad. All you need is a set course and a sense of adventure. Think unconventionally and consider alternative uses for imported details. For example, Asian temple doors make wonderful room separators and headboards. African drums create unique nightstands and accent tables. Beaded shawls and embroidered textiles fabricate fascinating pillows, draperies, and table runners. Tribal rugs make head-turning blankets. Just keep in mind that this is one room in which you can set your imagination free. Liberally display pieces gathered from travels. Paint the room with rambunctious color. Defy the norm.

PAGE 36
In a stylistic space like the exotic bedroom, make every item earn its keep. Each has the power to add significantly to the room's unique flavor. Here, beautiful flooring and ceiling treatments frame distinctively finished furnishings. The Asian-influenced bedding contributes to the South Pacific flavor of the décor, and the angled placement of the furnishing adds to the room's unconventional appeal.

LEFT
A collection of intriguing accessories creates an air of mystery in this enchanting bedroom. Iridescent silks, embroidered fabrics, and deep spice tones add to the room's mystique.

OPPOSITE
This exotic retreat enlists a lavish and imaginative canopy treatment that drapes yards upon yards of exquisite imported silks. The Moroccan theme flourishes with rich spicy colors, a harem of decorative pillows, and metallic accents throughout.

OPPOSITE UPPER LEFT
Unconventional latticework shutters turn this bedroom's windows into a stylistic and exotic work of art. Their natural finish complements the room's other accents including a rustic pottery lamp, potted yucca, and sheer drapes on the canopy bed.

OPPOSITE LOWER LEFT
A highly stylized screen creates a magical backdrop for a display of rustic pottery. The inclusion of the contemporary light fixture emphasizes the earthy texture of the jars and the heavy carvings of the furniture.

LEFT
Many cultures use unique carvings and woodwork to put their own signature of style on distinctive furnishings. Incorporating these pieces into your décor instantly imparts the flavor of the land from which it came. This magnificent bedroom is brimming with decoratively carved pieces that are wonderfully balanced by the colors and patterns of a custom rug, beamed ceiling, and unadorned plastered walls.

COCOON

A beautiful bedroom is like a cocoon, enclosing its inhabitants in comfort and style. This cocoon is formed by the surfaces of the room —its floors underfoot, the surrounding walls, and the ceiling above. Together they form the basis of the room's character and become the backdrop for its furnishings and accents. Decoratively detailed, they can enrich the space with a wealth of color, texture, and pattern which, when spun together, create a look that is unique and personal.

To neglect any one of these surfaces is to sacrifice the beauty of the bedroom. Certainly, unadorned floors and walls can appear chic in some settings; however, in most, they make the room's décor look temporary and short-lived. The same holds true of ceilings. Bare ceilings make an otherwise well-decorated space appear bottom heavy. It can look as if gravity pulled all the magic downward, leaving the upper portion of the space empty and barren. Simply said, beautifully detailed surfaces set the stage for an engaging bedroom. Consider this as you spin the cocoon of your own distinctively styled space.

As you jump out of bed and start your day, how does your bedroom floor greet you? Does it wake you with plush carpeting, smooth wood, or cool stone? Does it mute the sound of your movements or echo your every step? Does it offer a visual wealth of texture, pattern, and color or is it a monochromatic backdrop supporting detail found elsewhere in the room? We are more in touch with the bedroom floor than the room's other surfaces. We experience its texture, temperature, and tone with every step we take. More often than not, we encounter these characteristics with bare or stocking feet. For this reason, comfort is paramount when selecting just the right surface treatment for the bedroom floor. All materials—wood, marble, carpeting, and woven rugs to name a few—provide tactile sensations that affect the pleasure of walking across a bedroom floor. Consider this when you make your flooring decisions. These same materials also make very distinctive style statements. Some favor period looks while others complement contemporary, traditional, or regional décors. Factor the style quotient

FLOORS

into your decision process as well. With comfort and style in hand, or underfoot in this case, the bedroom floor invites unbridled detail and design that lays a fabulous foundation for the personality and enjoyment of the entire room.

Today's bedroom floors are no longer hiding under the bed. Beautifully detailed, they are the foundation upon which the room is built, literally and figuratively. Richly stained woods complement period as well as contemporary looks. Assorted stones and marbles offer elegance, rustic charm, and the essence of faraway places. Each of these is available in a variety of colors and dimensions and can be laid in endless patterns and combinations. Area rugs, from heirloom Orientals to modern abstracts, decorate the floor like paintings on a gallery's walls. They also add spots of comfort to hard cold surfaces. Of course wall-to-wall carpet provides a plane of plushness and texture-rich color at every step. Additional surfaces like bamboo, cork, and leather are additional stylish alternatives. Beyond comfort, noise level, and maintenance, there are no other criteria outside of pure style and creativity that you need to consider when selecting the perfect bedroom flooring. Set your imagination free.

PAGE 45
Like lily pads floating on a pond's surface, these circular rugs float across the bedroom's floor, creating eye-catching focal points on the wooden surface. This handsome room took the magic one step further and repeated the rug's ring-like motif on the lower portion of the lightly puddled drapes.

BELOW
When you plan to incorporate a large area rug in a bedroom, it is best to create or select it before proceeding with other design decisions. As this stunning guestroom demonstrates, an area rug is like a brilliant underfoot canvas and can provide the direction for the color and pattern play of the rest of the room.

OPPOSITE
Texture and pattern deliver layers of interest to a room. The carpet of this sophisticated master suite lays the foundation for this room's design direction as its tone-on-tone pattern is brilliantly repeated on the texture-rich upholstered bed and occasional chairs.

To give a floor instant character, turn to area rugs. They can give a room an immediate shot of color, texture, and pattern. Be creative—consider angled placement, layering one rug upon another, and using assorted styles in a single space. Area rugs offer flexibility in design and can be changed to create seasonal looks. They soften the sounds in a room framed by hard surfaces. Of course, they furnish plush and warm footing with every step you take.

THIS PAGE
The beauty of area rugs lies in their multiple forms and finishes. From exquisite Orientals, tribal kilims, and geometric abstracts to animal skins, painted canvases, and natural sisal, there is a type and style for every well-designed bedroom.

A star-filled sky, a canopy of fluttering leaves, or fluffy clouds moving across the horizon, . . . to fall asleep beneath any of these is one of life's simplest pleasures. It is also the inspiration that has transformed characterless bedroom ceilings into sky-high surfaces alive with detail. What do you see when you gaze upward from your bed? If it is a blank ceiling, you may be missing a wonderful opportunity to add unique style to your bedroom. From a simple application of color to an elaborate fresco or series of timber beams, there are limitless ways to accent the overhead surface with character. Architecture, too, can shape the ceiling with vaulting, contoured coving,

CEILINGS

and angled planes, to name a few treatments. Light fixtures also can be used to draw the eye upward as can ceiling-height stencils and shapely moldings. Of course, fabric-tented canopy beds create a second ceiling above the bed that invites additional imaginative overhead treatments. When it comes to the bedroom ceiling, the sky is the limit for the endless ways to color it with unique personality and style.

Like an hourglass in which all the sand has run to the bottom, so it is with rooms where a ceiling is left unadorned. All the detail sits at the base, making the space look bottom heavy and empty up above. However, a decorated ceiling can balance the room, filling it with character. It can also shape the experience of the space. As you enter a bedroom with a detailed ceiling, your eye is drawn upward. If color is employed, a darker shade makes the ceiling seem closer, creating a more intimate feel for the space. Lighter shades send the ceiling skyward, making the room more airy and spacious. A coat of paint is the simplest way to apply interest. Other treatments—metal, wood, faux finishes, stone—provide pattern and texture as well as color. Skylights, beams, domes, and moldings are architectural details that produce permanent impact. Ceiling fans and dangling mobiles can act like jewels that accessorize a ceiling with distinct character and personality. And lighting—it works magic in the bedroom. Lamps and torchères place pools of light on the ceiling's surface and tracked halogens, hanging chandeliers, and well-placed spotlights detail with their forms and finishes.

PAGE 50
A large-domed ceiling, magnificently finished in gold, crowns a bedroom with grandeur and Old World beauty. Its generous circumference makes the spacious room appear to be even larger.

RIGHT
Elaborate moldings and distinctive trims enrich this bedroom ceiling with timeless elegance. While these intricate features were laboriously hand-carved, today's versions are readily available in preformed plaster, foam, and wood varieties.

FAR RIGHT
Loft living displays the home's functional elements like pieces of art. On the ceiling of this city-chic suite, raw wood, pipes, and ductwork are left exposed to exaggerate the edgy, urban design.

Bedroom ceiling treatments can range from restrained to riotous. Paint is the simplest treatment, adding instant color and depth to the surface. If there are irregularities in the ceiling, a glossy paint will exaggerate them and a flat paint will subdue them. Wallpaper, fabric, and trompe l'oeil also can be used to mask ceiling flaws and enrich the surface with pattern and scenery. Take care not to overwhelm the ceiling with these treatments. Architectural features—moldings, beams, vigas, domes, coffered woodwork, skylights—are more-elaborate treatments that dramatically contribute to the style of the bedroom. Because they can often become major focal points in the room, they should be considered when incorporating other high-impact details in the space. Too many dramatic features can become visually overwhelming.

UPPER LEFT
Raw-timber vigas and sculpted ceilings add immeasurable character to this stunning suite. Well-designed lighting is incorporated to provide functional and highly dramatic illumination of the overhead architectural details.

LOWER RIGHT
The ceiling of this Old World bedroom greatly contributes to the strength of its style. Dark rough-hewn beams, a scrolled-iron chandelier, and an imaginatively draped canopy, all spectacularly detail the surface crowning the room with unmistakable panache.

A man's style is his mind's voice.

Ralph Waldo Emerson

ABOVE
Dark rich beams and carved corbel accents add
timeless character to the space while visually drawing
the lofty ceiling downward. They make the spacious
room more intimate and comforting.

If you have hit the wall trying to add character and personality to your bedroom, look no further. The walls of the room present one of the best opportunities to bring the room to life. They alone can set the tone for the style of the entire space, enriching it with texture, color, and pattern. Further, because they comprise so much of the bedroom's surface space, any change in their appearance, no matter how minor, can

WALLS

dramatically affect the room's ambience. Brilliant and subtle tones are captured in soft washes, mottled Venetian plasters, and solid planes of color. Frescos, trompe l'oeil, rich wallpapers, and fabrics introduce a play of pattern and scenery. Unique materials—metal, glass, exotic woods—imbue the room with unforgettable drama. Architectural details—niches, moldings, wainscoting, arches—become accents that can turn the most common wall into something extraordinary. Each detail has the ability to add undeniable character to the room and to affect its mood and the way the space of the room is perceived. Certainly, white walls have their place; however, considering the many other options available, you no longer need to feel that your back is up against the wall when creating the style of this all-important surface.

Consider the rules of wardrobing. We all know a black dress is slenderizing, patterns are attention-grabbing, and stripes are powerful in their ability to make a figure appear long and lean or a mile wide, depending on the direction in which the stripes run. These same rules apply to surface treatments worn by today's bedroom walls. Just as a dark suit slims a figure, deeply toned walls have a similar effect on a room's space, compressing it spatially. They make it appear smaller and more intimate. Light colors have the opposite effect, expanding a room and making it brighter and airier. Patterns can be wonderfully thematic and add textural interest. Small-scale patterns are subtle and spatially affect the room much like a solid color. Large patterns, on the other hand, are statement making and add immediate dimension to the wall. They should be used cautiously. Like a busy floral-print dress on a woman, large prints can overwhelm a bedroom if not applied judiciously. Mirrored walls expand a bedroom's space, visually doubling the decorative effect of every detail reflected in their surfaces. High-gloss paints, shiny materials, and luminous fabrics also make a room seem larger as light careens from their surfaces and brightens the room.

PAGE 56
Pastoral views of the Italian countryside are brought to life in this bedroom's wonderful trompe l'oeil treatment. Alone, this wall detail single-handedly sets the decorative theme and color story of the entire room.

PAGE 57
This rustically rich Old World bedroom features a two-toned paint treatment that warms the space and highlights its architectural features. Darker colors were historically used on the lower portion of the walls to obscure soil and markings inflicted upon them.

OPPOSITE
Mirrors work like magic in the bedroom as they expand its space visually and double the impact of its decorative details.

UPPER RIGHT
Small patterns add subtle dimension to a room and are naturally thematic in their motifs and prints. This beautifully designed room contrasts a softly patterned wallpaper with a fabric-padded screen with wonderful results.

LOWER RIGHT
Color is one of the simplest and most expressive ways to imbue character and emotion upon the bedroom. Red Venetian plaster brings drama and a deep-toned intimacy to this high-impact space.

Unlike a kitchen, bathroom, dining room, or family room, the bedroom is not subjected to the excessive humidity, the splattering of food and water, or the wear and tear common to those high-traffic spaces. For this reason, the practical considerations for detailing the bedroom walls are few. Treatments unfeasible in other rooms are entirely at home here. Be imaginative and indulgent in your choices when dressing your bedroom walls. Silken fabrics can adorn them with their elegance while softening the sounds of the space. Porous stone, brick, and plaster bring distinctive texture and a taste of Old World styling. Hand-painted scenery, a gallery wall of framed images, draping textiles, natural-fiber papers, panels of wood, glass, and mirrors are other stylish and viable treatments for this private sanctuary.

RIGHT
Fabric-covered walls render a bedroom richly opulent and beautiful. The weave and sheen of this suite's silk-covered walls imparts an understated elegance upon the space.

OPPOSITE
A pair of stone-framed antique doors details this bedroom's walls while creating a weighty and wonderful focal point for the room. Distinctive bedroom wall treatments often double as one-of-a-kind headboards.

As a wall feature in a bedroom, the fireplace is one of the most demanding focal points and indulgent design elements there is. Its distinctive form bridges the architecture and style of the space. A broad-shouldered mantel and stone hearth make a declaration of tradition and grandeur. An unadorned box floating in a white wall or framed by stainless steel and glass sets the tone for a minimalist and modern décor. Each element of the fireplace—its opening, box, chimney, mantel, hearth, andirons, tools—provides a wonderful opportunity to detail the bedroom with your personal statement of style.

LEFT
As much a work of art as a working wall feature, this stunning fireplace is fashioned from a sculpted mix of unusual materials. The broad panes of glass that frame the fireplace on each side heighten its decorative impact on the room.

OPPOSITE
Created with the belief that less is more, this high-style bedroom incorporates a large unembellished fireplace that resembles a piece of minimalist art. The raised firebox is well suited for the bedroom as it makes the flames and burning embers visible while one is lying in bed.

What is more romantic than a fireplace in a bedroom? Its dancing flames can illuminate a room with a light and warmth that are intoxicating. The allure of spending cold winter nights under lofty bedding while glowing embers lull you to sleep is like a dream. Weekend mornings, lounging in front of a fire with a paper and coffee are equally enticing. As the bedroom's mood-maker, a fireplace is unmatched.

LOWER LEFT
Hand-painted tiles can dress a fireplace surround with undeniable character and color. The zigzag pattern of this Western-style feature mimics the finish of the two talavera pots that accent it.

UPPER RIGHT
The fireplace is such a strong decorative feature that it is often incorporated in the bedroom even when it is inoperable. The facade of this charming period fireplace suggests a working feature even though it is purely decorative. Its painted mantel and hearth provide a wonderful focal point as well as a place to display cherished accessories.

OPPOSITE
As a focal point, the bedroom fireplace is unsurpassed. The arrangement of the room's furniture is often fixed upon it. The fireplace of this richly detailed bedroom is set at an angle so it can be seen from anywhere in the room. The leather sleigh bed, chair, and ottoman are positioned to take advantage of the angled setting.

BEDS

The bed is the namesake of the room we sleep in, . . . and with good reason. It is the bedroom's most basic and essential element, its most prevalent focal point, and the one piece that is most likely to set the tone and style of the entire space. Its dimension, design, dressings, and placement all direct and dictate the flavor of the bedroom. A large four-poster carved bed dressed with a full canopy and centered in the space is like a luxurious room within a room. Its decorative presence is commanding. A minimalist futon, while also making an equally strong design statement, leaves the space open, airy, and a perfect setting for a more modern or eclectic mix of design details. However you decide to define the look of your bedroom, whatever name you give its style, the bed is the first and most formidable place to begin the detailing of the space.

Have you ever noticed how the frame that surrounds a priceless oil painting or piece of modern photography can either enhance or diminish the beauty of the work of art? The frame itself is a statement of style that positively

FRAMES

or negatively affects the style of that which it borders. The same is true of a bed frame. Its overall design impacts the decorative appeal of the entire bed and the room in which it sits.

To many people, the frame is the bed; when in fact, the bed actually consists of a mattress set linens, and pillows as well. Together, these many elements of the modern bed should work together to create a cohesive statement of style. The frame, however, is the ideal starting point for creating your version of the perfect bed. Do you favor a lofty carved canopy that is draped and decorated with copious bedclothes? Maybe you prefer a stainless-steel sleigh bed fitted with crisp and tailored textiles. These are just a couple of the endless possibilities. In any case, once you determine the direction of your bedroom's style, the bed frame can serve as the singular most important piece of furniture to help you create the look of your dreams.

In many bedrooms, the bed frame actually shapes the essence of the space. By removing or replacing it, the feel and style of the room is totally changed. A bed frame has many characteristics—size, shape, finish—that define its style. The size or dimension of a frame directly affects the spatial perception of the bedroom. Large canopy beds can fill a voluminous bedroom making it more cozy and comfortable. They can be left unadorned to emphasize their lines and finish, or be heavily draped with fabric to fill and soften the room. The more heavily draped, the more they dominate the room. For smaller bedrooms, low-profile designs such as sleigh, platform, or classic brass beds can add incredible style without overwhelming the room spatially. They are well suited for rooms with low ceilings and limited square footage. The color and finish of a frame can also affect the way a room is perceived. The more the bed frame contrasts with its surroundings—a dark frame in a light-colored room for example—the more it masters over the room and absorbs its space. The opposite is true of frames that are finished similarly to the room's other elements.

UPPER LEFT
This large-scale bed makes a powerful architectural statement in the spacious room. Tall, beautifully carved posts emphasize the height of the frame as well as the room's ceilings. The scrolled-iron canopy is left unadorned to play up its beauty and keep the space open and light.

LOWER LEFT
The bed frame wields enormous power to shape the look and feel of the bedroom. A perfect example, this log-framed canopy defines the Mountain style of this master suite with its weighty build and natural finish. Plush bedding softens the timber's roughness.

OPPOSITE
A frame that is beautifully styled is better simply dressed to allow its lines and design to prevail. This stunning iron bed helps to spatially define the area of the bed without blocking the view seen through the French doors.

71

*The bed comprehends our whole life, for we were born in
it, we live in it, and we shall die in it.*

Guy de Maupassant

OPPOSITE AND ABOVE

For years, canopy beds have ruled supreme as the most stylish
of bed frames. Not any more. Today's assortment of high-style
sleigh beds, horizontal headboards, and one-of-a-kind
sculpture-like frames pack enough punch to make the low-
profile frame a winner in bedrooms of all types.

Is your bed on your home's best dressed list? Do its linens draw admiring glances each time someone enters the room? If not, you may be overlooking the single most dramatic and one of the easiest ways to create a one-of-a-kind look for the room. Just as they say clothes make the man, so it is true that the linens make the bed. They can take a common uninspired frame and dress-it-to-the-nines, making the bed the stylish

LINENS

star of the room. Conversely, a beautiful bed garbed with tired sheets and blankets can appear dowdy and dull. The power of bed linens to make or break the style of the room is enormous. Whether you favor the cachet of couture luxury linens or ogle the beautiful options of off-the-rack bedding pieces, there are endless ways to attire your bed so it becomes the model of perfection in the bedroom suite.

How do you make your bed? Whatever design direction you determine for your private sanctuary, today's linens have evolved into an art form that offers endless ways to create a stylish personalized look for your bed. There are many elements to a well-dressed bed. Starting with a dust ruffle or mattress cover that dresses and disguises exposed railing and box spring, you can further attire the mattress with a topper. A pad of wool, quilted cotton, or foam, as well as a luscious feather bed can be used to top the mattress with sumptuous comfort. Beautiful fitted and top sheets come next, followed by a blanket, bed-spread, coverlet, or duvet-covered comforter. Sleeping pillows are available in a variety of sizes and qualities including down, fiber-filled, and foam, that can be gowned in your choice of lovely covers and shams. They are joined by an onslaught of decorative pieces including neck rolls, boudoir and accent pillows, wonderfully woven throws, and daring drapes. Combined, coordinated, or mixed and matched, these pieces invite you to give your personal style free reign as you transform your basic bed into a refuge of comfort and irresistible beauty.

PAGE 75
Wrapped in luxury, this dreamy bedding ensemble entices with exquisite pillows, a sheer-draped canopy, and a soft-as-a-whisper duvet. By using a mixture of unique and luxurious fabrics as well as distinctive trims, these monochromatic bed linens bring a wonderfully romantic look to this canopy bed.

OPPOSITE
Like an elegant throne, this stunning bed is dressed in velvet and accessorized with a mixture of beautiful floral-patterned pillows. The high-backed headboard is an ideal backdrop for the three large Euro shams and additional accessory pillows.

RIGHT
Clean-lined and sophisticated, this leather bed is per-fectly suited for a straightforward approach to its attire. The pillows are stacked rather than layered, the spread is flat and tailored, and the limited patterns are geo-metric and simple. A luxurious throw creates a touch of drama and glamour.

*Simplification is the
glory of expression.*

Walt Whitman

Attractive bed linens need not be opulent or
excessively detailed. Sometimes the beauty of an
item is found in its simplicity. These beds are
dressed with serenely styled with softly colored
linens, plain or muted patterned fabrics, and
limited decorative pillows. The effect is relaxed
and comforting.

The bed has become the focus of some of the world's most famous fashion designers. They dress it like a shapely runway model, using the finest materials available. Termed as "luxury bed linens," these specialty bedding lines feature fabrics from the finest mills in the world. Egyptian cotton, Italian linen, silk, high-tech fibers, luxurious blends, lambs' wool, as well as matelassé and sateen fabrics are among the textiles offering over-the-top indulgence to discerning dreamers. In fine linens, quality is measured by the thread count—the number of threads per square inch of fabric. A 180- to 200-thread count is standard while 350 and above is considered luxurious. The higher-thread-count materials are softer, more comfortable, and longer lasting. Lavish embroidery, beading, monogramming, and trim often embellish these fine linens.

OPPOSITE UPPER LEFT
Monochromatic bed linens lend this space a feel of sophistication and glamour. Additionally, the bedding's exquisite details and workmanship become even more apparent in single-color styling.

OPPOSITE LOWER LEFT
Decorative pillows adorn a bed like beautiful art does a wall. They color it with texture and tone that is ever changeable, thus bringing flexibility to its look and feel.

LEFT
Bed linens instill texture and tone to a bedroom interior. This fashion-forward bedroom uses the bed skirt, shams, and decorative pillows to add shots of vivid shades, while the more-fixed pieces—sheets, sleeping pillows, duvet—establish a more permanent hue. This allows the home owner to change the overall color story of the ensemble by replacing only a few of its pieces.

Centuries ago, the headboard was a symbol of status. Today it is a symbol of style. It crowns the bed with its unique character and personality. Creating a focal point for the overall room, it draws the eye to the bed and produces a backdrop for its distinctive pillows and linens. Its scale can affect the perception of the space as it adds

HEADBOARDS

vertical as well as horizontal dimension to the room. Its silhouette strongly dictates the direction of the room's design. A tufted-fabric headboard of toile is timeless and traditional, a vertical slab of stone is rustic, and freeform sculpted steel is ultracontemporary. Whatever the shape and material of this favored feature, it can transform an unadorned bed into a monument of architecture and art.

Today's headboard is like a magnet for imaginative detail and ingenious design. In most rooms, it acts as a work of art above the bed. The headboard treatment can run the gamut from makeshift to magnificent. A panel of beautiful fabric or a pleated drape hung behind the bed is an easy way to infuse color and softness to the wall. Suspended quilts, woven-reed shades, or sheets of sheer muslin are other options that add character and unique detail. A uniquely shaped piece of wood upholstered with a distinctive textile or a tent-like fabric feature that drapes over the head of the bed can be dramatic and beautiful. Architectural items—old scrolled gates, iron-studded doors, a screen of stained-glass windows—are additional ways to transform an ordinary bed into an extraordinary sculpture. These and endless other ideas prove there are unlimited methods to replace the traditional headboard with stylish stand-ins overflowing with creativity and distinctive character.

UPPER RIGHT
A framework of vividly colored fabric panels and black-and-white photos creates a wonderful contemporary headboard for this simply styled room.

LOWER RIGHT
A boxy corona and pleated, paneled drapes create a stunning character-filled alcove for this ornately decorated bed.

OPPOSITE
Upholstery is one of the simplest and most versatile ways to infuse the headboard with pattern, texture, and color. The fabric used can be repeated in the room's bedding and upholstered seating pieces. The headboard can be beautifully pleated or tufted as well as trimmed in endless braids, decorative tapes, and tassels. Its shape can range from rigidly squared to softly curved and anything in between.

To create a dramatic head-board with unforgettable impact, think beyond the norm. Introduce unexpected materials, imaginative treatments, and surprising details. Because this feature is purely decorative and not limited by practical considerations, the sky is the limit when developing its one-of-a-kind design.

RIGHT
An architectural alcove just deep enough to house a pair of antique iron gates creates a stunning and unique headboard in this rustic desert home.

FAR RIGHT
A tufted leather-covered wall suggests a floor-to-ceiling headboard where there is none. Its rich patina, harlequin pattern, and stunning carved-wood frame defines the room's Old World beauty. Its substantial size and dramatic detail make it the primary focal point in the space.

BEDFELLOWS

Once upon a time, the bedroom was used solely for sleeping and dressing. Its furnishings consisted of a bed and a single storage piece—perhaps a dresser or simple bedside table. Today, as the bedroom has evolved into the home's private sanctuary, its furnishing requirements have also changed. The room's bedfellows—the furniture, lighting, and accessories—have become as rich in design and detail as those found in the home's showiest spots. Exquisitely crafted chests, beautiful bureaus, and stately armoires team with luxuriously upholstered seating pieces, creating an indulgent chamber in which to retreat. Lighting has outgrown overhead bulbs and paired lamps on matching nightstands. Now pieces ranging from elegant chandeliers to mood-setting sconces are used to cast a glorious glow over the wonderfully appointed room. Of course, cherished accessories that truly personalize the space are gathered and grouped to showcase the personality and taste of the room's inhabitants.

Whatever style you select for your bedroom, the lines, designs, and details of its furnishings can help you achieve the look you crave. Finishes to forms, moldings to metalwork, they all play a part in the panache that the furniture brings to the room. In a contemporary space, smooth leather dresses the sleek silhouettes of a high-style chair or chrome-framed chaise. Beautifully finished storage pieces devoid of excess moldings and hardware accentuate the room's minimalist direction. Low-standing platform beds and glass-topped accent pieces complete the space. For the traditionalist, furnishings are more richly detailed with heavy carvings, finely polished woods, and turned legs. Top-grain leather and stately tapestries are accented with ornate braids and brass nail-head trims. Seating is plush and overstuffed. Eclectic and transitionally styled spaces bring together multicultural elements and imaginative blends of materials and styles. An interplay from stone to straw, wood to wicker, forms dynamically designed pieces that fill the space with a unique and personal style.

PAGE 91
An eclectic medley of streamlined chairs, a heavily carved armoire, stone-topped chests, and a hand-forged wrought-iron bed shapes the multicultural mixture of this spectacular master suite.

UPPER LEFT
The East-meets-West details of this softly styled bedroom are reflected in a beautifully carved armoire and freshly fashioned canopy bed. A mixture of finishes and forms shape the look.

LOWER LEFT
Contemporary bedrooms need not be hard and sleek. A combination of uncluttered lines, texture-rich materials, and fashion-forward forms can create a stylish alternative to a cold, minimalist design.

OPPOSITE
The character of this stunning bedroom is shaped by a series of streamlined built-ins purposefully lacking ornamentation and hardware. Richly grained wood and smooth sumptuous leather further harmonize to emphasize the modern appeal of the room.

The bedside table is the workhorse of the modern bedroom. It hosts the necessities of the space—lamps, alarm clocks, books, telephones, pictures—and keeps them within reach of the room's slumbering inhabitants. Once predictably embodied in matching boxes framing both sides of the bed, today's nightstands have morphed into imaginative and intriguing pieces that color the room with the personal styles and tastes of those who use it.

OPPOSITE
Clockwise from upper left: (UL) A stone-topped nightstand provides ample storage and features additional surface with a pull-out shelf. (UR) Perfectly sized for bedside placement, this classically styled, marble-topped table is ideal for displaying beautiful accessories. (LL) Boxy chests make wonderful nightstands, offering plentiful storage capacity as well as unique and distinctive styling. (LR) In today's multi-purpose bedroom suite, the desk performs double duty as a wonderful workstation and as a bedside table that is beautiful and spacious.

LEFT
With a little imagination, the most unique piece can be transformed into a modern-day bedside table. This antique cart is perfectly suited for the job, offering plenty of display space as well as a height and styling that complement the richly carved bed.

Well-designed bedrooms are like a work of art. Their stunning surfaces, furnishings, and bedding form the room's style and shape its beauty. However, without accessories, the composition seems unfinished. Accessories are the finishing touches—the cherished objects that color a bedroom with personality and wash it with character. In the bedroom, they tint the space at

ACCESSORIES

every turn—portraits and pictures enrich the walls, decorative pillows and throws accent the bed, lamps and lighting pieces brighten the area and define it with their shapely forms. Most of all, unexpected and singular items impart the personality of the bedroom's inhabitants upon the space—from pictures to unique collectibles, architectural remnants to fresh florals.

The bedroom is truly your own private refuge. Why not embellish it with pieces that have special meaning to you? After all, they will be the last thing you see before falling asleep and the first thing you enjoy when you awake. Be creative and daring with the items you choose. Surround yourself with personal collections, individual pieces acquired from memorable travels, and treasured objects of immeasurable sentiment. Keep in mind their influence upon the style of the room. They can impact it with their colors, shapes, sizes, and textures. In modern bedrooms, less is more. Be disciplined in the choice and positioning of the few items you display. In eclectic and more traditional décors, numerous objects create a wonderful way to enhance the bedroom, as long as their placement is visually appealing and well thought out. In any case, no matter what design direction you favor, accessories are the key to finishing the well-designed bedroom so that it reflects your passions and uniquely presents your personal style.

Because the bedroom is so personal, there is no better place to display a collection of items that has special meaning to you. Collectibles are defined by the passions, interests, and senti-mentalities of their owner. The shapes and sizes of collectibles vary, their visual strengths differ. To effectively display them, here are some useful guidelines. For a large group of similar pieces, select a common characteristic of the items and use that as the criterion that bonds them together. Whether this common quality is color, material, age, or item type, it will serve as the basis for a unified and appealing display. For a series of identical pieces, it is effective to position them in a strict and orderly fashion. For a small group of somewhat dissimilar items, a less structured display of odd-numbered pieces is visually pleasing. Never scatter a collection around a room. It loses its focus, and sense of importance. Finally, be bold in what you collect and what you display. While groupings of family photos, books, and grooming instruments are familiar in a bedroom setting, any collection that is special to you—boxes to bottles, baubles to balls—has a place in your private retreat.

OPPOSITE UPPER LEFT
Beautifully colored glass balls are "eye candy" as they sparkle and shine on a bedroom table. As a collection, their loose arrangement favors a casually styled room.

OPPOSITE LOWER LEFT
A collection of blanc de chin pottery pieces top a bedroom's contemporary glass-front cabinet. While color and material unifies the group, their different shapes and sizes make them best displayed asymmetrically.

OPPOSITE LOWER RIGHT
A favorite among collectors, beautiful boxes make a wonderful display in the bedroom. Their unique materials, rich finishes, and assorted sizes, styles, and shapes make them interesting individually and spectacular when grouped.

LEFT
Stunning Chinese porcelains create a dramatic grouping on this bedroom's antique chest. Their blue-and-white color and delicate patterns are wonderfully repeated in the room's linens and upholstered armchair.

Tabletops and dressers are not the only surfaces that host the presentation of accessories and art in the bedroom. Walls invite the decorative strength of these items, as well. Beautifully framed oils and photography are naturals here, but they are not the only options. Imaginatively displayed items including tapestries, window frames, iron gates, carvings, architectural artifacts, and clothing can make a dramatic and unforgettable statement of style in the space. When displaying wall art, be thoughtful of its placement height. Because much of the time is spent either sitting or lying down in this room, the height at which the piece is viewed is often lower. In that case, the image should also be positioned lower as well. For instance, art hung over a nightstand should be placed at eye level while sitting or lying in bed. On the other hand, a piece viewed while standing or entering the room is more likely to favor a higher position on a wall.

UPPER LEFT
A wall-mounted kimono creates a unique and exquisite focal point for this bedroom. Its color and design accent the room brilliantly.

LOWER RIGHT
Scenic screens and timeless oils infuse this room with unmistakable romance. Used like a mobile wall, screens can be effective in hiding or disguising a bedroom's work or exercise area or in simply making a bold statement of style.

OPPOSITE
A large, abstract painting is the primary focal point of this modern bedroom. It provides visual height that balances the low-profile sleigh bed and adds depth and dimension to the otherwise blank wall.

A room hung with pictures is a room
hung with thoughts.

Joshua Reynolds

*You begin with a group of objects and then you build a
room like a glove to hold them.*

Gaillard F. Ravenel

Have fun with your bedroom display—be bold and daring. Select items that make you smile and add a touch of whimsy to the space. Stage the items in interesting interplays of color, shape, size, and texture. Mix functional pieces such as lamps and books with decorative clusters of crystals and stylish sculptures. Stack small boxes or books to create platforms for displaying a prized bronze or piece of pottery. Stand a small painting on top of the table or chest rather than hanging it above the piece; use it as the back-drop for a composition. Consider using two candle lamps rather than one and position one of them slightly in front of the other. Complement square-cornered items with smooth and rounded pieces. Place a mirror behind your staging to double its visual impact. Whatever pieces you treasure, utilize their common qualities and play off of their dissimilarities. Remember that accessorizing is an art, not a science. Trial and error is the recipe for success in staging the accessories of an inspired bedroom.

OPPOSITE AND LEFT
Placement is everything in this simple, yet stunning bedroom. The bed and large yucca frame the desk like theater curtains frame a stage. The desktop accessories are arranged to highlight the beauty of each individual piece while creating a cohesive and dramatic composition. The centered mirror anchors the grouping; the lamps provide height and the books give the arrangement weight. The glass balls add color, sparkle, and the tranquil effect of rounded spheres.

A sconce created from alabaster, an antique lamp shaded with shantung silk, or a chandelier with outstretched arms sparkling with light, . . . today's bedroom lighting has become sculpture-like in its form and magical in its ability to set the ambience of the room. Stunning fixtures of all styles feature imaginative designs and rich finishes. They hang from ceilings, adorn walls, accessorize chests, and glow from behind architectural details. Some illuminate the overall room, some brighten its work areas, and still others pour romantic pools of light throughout the space. Great lighting is a perfect blend of both form and function. And, of course, without light, none of the room's other rich detailing could be seen or enjoyed.

LIGHTS & MIRRORS

Mirrors work with light to reflect the beauty of the bedroom and, in many cases, double the drama of its design and detailing. Traditionally, mirrors have been part of the boudoir as they hung over vanities and dressing tables. Today, they are also used wall-to-wall to visually expand the overall space, placed over dressers and fireplaces as accent pieces, and displayed in handheld pieces as part of vintage grooming collections. Exquisitely framed and delightfully detailed, they are like pieces of art. Thoughtfully placed, they are one of the most effective and hardest working accessories used to decorate today's bedroom.

A bedroom's fixtures should combine three types of light—general lighting that illuminates the overall space, ambient lighting that adds drama and decorative detailing, and task lighting that aids reading and writing in the room. This mixture makes the room work. It can be accomplished by incorporating a combination of sconces, table lamps, floor lamps, hanging pieces, up-lights, and spots. Beyond the type of light that each of these fixtures provides is the style the fixture contributes through its form and finish. Bases of wood, metal, or ceramic can be crowned with splendid shades of paper, copper, fabric, mica, or even bone to name a few. There has never been such an assortment of stunning shades available, and a new shade is one of the easiest ways to put a new face on an old lamp. Displaying a mixture of dissimilar lamps and fixtures in a room adds interest and intrigue. Because the bedroom is all about ambience, do not forget to incorporate dimmers in your lighting plan. And, of course, keep plenty of candles on hand. They are not only one of the oldest ways to illuminate the boudoir, but also, they are the most romantic.

PAGE 105
To instantly enlarge a bedroom, cover one of its walls with mirrors. This tactic not only increases the visual space of the room, it also doubles its light. In this small, mirrored bedroom, a mixture of spots and table lamps warm it at night while shuttered sunlight brightens it throughout the day.

UPPER LEFT
Matching table lamps are symmetrically placed to complement the twin beds of this guestroom. Sticking with a clean and simple look keeps this small space from being overwhelmed with detail.

LOWER LEFT
To ensure enough overall lighting for this bedroom, spots are strategically placed in its ceiling. They can be softened with the simple adjustment of a dimmer switch. Shaded table lamps are incorporated as shapely accessories that, when illuminated, contribute greatly to the ambience of the space.

OPPOSITE
Architecturally arresting lamps dramatically frame this bed with their brilliant forms and finishes. They provide abundant reading light and can be turned to highlight the art above the bed.

The bedroom is a haven for beautiful mirrors. From a practical standpoint, they help the room's inhabitants get dressed for the day. They can seemingly expand the room spatially when used to cover one of its walls. When placed behind a display of beautiful objects, they magically multiply the pieces and increase their decorative impact upon the room. In addition, mirrors also perform like head-turning art. Their unique shapes and sizes, finely finished frames, and exquisite bevels, etchings, and surface treatments make them some of the most beautiful and appreciated accessories in the room.

OPPOSITE
A mirror makes a wonderful backdrop for a beautifully accessorized table. It adds light to the display and depth to its drama. The elaborate frame of this oval mirror complements the assorted filigreed picture frames as well as the ornately carved console.

UPPER RIGHT
A large framed mirror can create the impression of a window or passageway as it lures one into its reflection. This beautifully carved, wood-framed mirror casually stands on the floor to showcase the room's beauty

LOWER LEFT
Hung above a chest of drawers, a mirror can make straightening your tie or fixing your hair a snap. This mirror is perfectly sized to crown this bureau and its round frame accentuates the shape of the other accessories.

PURPOSE

Rare is the bedroom that is devoted solely to sleeping. After all, consider its evolution. Yesterday's practical space created entirely for sleeping and dressing has given way to uniquely designed, multipurpose master, guest, and children's bedrooms. Today's master suites perform not only as bedrooms but also as home offices, entertainment areas, exercise rooms, and lounges. They are created to satisfy the wants and needs of their owners and have become the home's most individual and self-indulgent room. Guestrooms are a haven for hospitality and often offer small studies and independent sitting areas. Children's rooms double as imaginative play spaces fashioned to grow with the little ones for whom they were designed. Adjoined rooms frequently double the functional strength of many bedrooms, offering laundry, hobby, dressing, outdoor living, and of course, bathing areas. Behind the development of today's multifaceted bedroom is the power of detail. Detail has single-handedly enabled this sleepy room to come alive in form and function and to evolve into one of the most active and purposeful rooms in the home.

The one word that best describes the perfect master bedroom is "personal." This space is the one room that is designed to cater to no one but you, its master. It is not created for show, does not open itself up for public display, and ideally indulges your personal interests and passions. It is uniquely yours. Your pleasure should be its focus. How would you describe your perfect bedroom? How would it perform for you?

MASTER SUITE

These are important questions to ask as you design and detail this personal refuge. Remember that today's master suite is rarely a room created solely for sleeping and dressing. As your private living room, it should accommodate any activities meaningful to you and make them more enjoyable. Keep in mind your determined purposes for the space and let them influence elements throughout the room—for example, make comfort the main ingredient in an off-the-bedroom sitting area—soft lighting, reachable tables, plush upholstery. Consider a hard flooring surface and a ceiling fan for an exercise space. Good lighting is a must for a quiet corner dedicated to reading or writing. The key is to focus on your needs and to indulge your style. If you do, you will have a one-of-a-kind master suite that reflects your personal taste and is wonderfully livable.

While every master bedroom is different, comfort remains the overriding theme for them all. Of course, each individual's interpretation of comfort differs. Some people find richly decorated, plush bedrooms ideal, while others prefer something modern, clean-lined, and somewhat sparse. The first step in creating the consummate master suite is to decide upon your definition of comfort. The next step is to put it to work. Because today's master bedroom is often large, it can be helpful to envision the room as a series of smaller, more distinct areas, . . . the lounging area, the sleeping area, and the TV area, for example. Furnish and design each area according to its function, but use decorative detail to provide continuity between them. This comes in many forms including common flooring material, wall color, overhead lighting fixtures, and the fabrics used throughout the space. Consider each element of detail that you layer upon the space as a common thread that ties the multifaceted room together.

PAGE 112
Shared spaces can be all the more beautiful when united by common detail. This multipurpose master suite features separate sleeping, working, and sitting areas but enlists dark woods, golden color tones, and a floating half-crescent-shaped ceiling treatment to fuse them together.

RIGHT
Texture and tone work hand-in-hand to detail this luxurious master bedroom. An interplay of luscious fabrics, all similar in color, create a subtle backdrop for the room's distinctive wood pieces and the spectacular desert view beyond.

OPPOSITE
There are many ways to define separate areas in the same room, furniture placement and multiple focal points are among the most powerful. This modern master bedroom designates the sitting area with plush upholstery and anchors it with a cylindrical fireplace. A large beautifully attired bed is the statement piece in the room's sleeping area. A wonderfully lighted sculpture-like ceiling and sophisticated wall treatments unite the two areas.

Where the good things are, there is home.

Euripides

Rest assured, the master bedroom is still primarily for quiet repose. Even though it may house areas for exercise, watching TV, or working at a desk, retreat and relaxation should prevail here. Elements and equipment that promote "outside interests" should be removable or easily disguised. For example, if you work at a desk in the bedroom, place the day's paperwork or bills in a drawer when you finish attending to them. If you have a treadmill or exercise mat in the space, return it to a closet or block it with a screen when you are finished. These and other intrusions on the relaxed nature of the room are not compatible with its calming effect. Instead, play up the indulgent and luxurious use of the space—breakfast in bed, long lingering naps, simple quiet escapes from the outside world.

OPPOSITE
Serene and nurturing, a bedroom dressed in white instantly washes away the worries of the day. This beautifully detailed suite mixes timeless antiques with the rustic charm of southwest living and wraps it all in a calming coat of white.

BELOW AND RIGHT
Never pass on the simpler pleasures in life. A master bedroom is an open invitation to sleeping late on weekends, taking breakfasts in bed, and simply escaping into its embrace when the need arises.

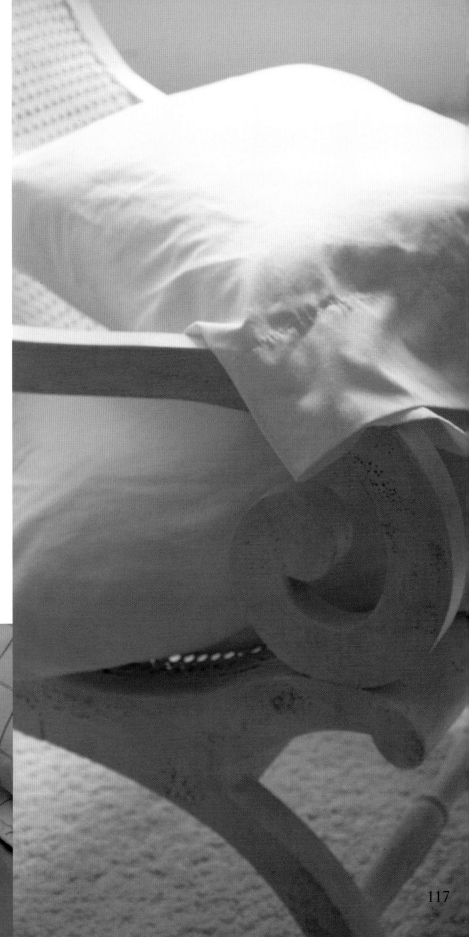

117

Who better to learn from about creating a wonderful guest room than those who make a living doing it? Who are they? . . . the ministers of comfort at luxury hotels, of course. It is their purpose in life to pamper and indulge their daily guests with everything imaginable. If you take your cues from these professionals, you just may have difficulty getting your guests to leave. The recipe to follow: detail, detail, detail. To pamper a visiting friend or family member, start with a serene and comforting setting—soft colors, sunny windows, uncluttered space. Good lighting is a must. Provide a comfortable mattress and dress it with luxury linens and sleeping pillows. Always keep extra pillows and blankets easily accessible. Position the bedside table so that it is easily reached and equip it with a clock, a lamp, and something to read. If room permits, create a cozy reading corner with a cushy chair, a shaded lamp, and a lap throw. Offer plenty of empty closet and drawer space and numerous matching hangers. Regarding the room's accessories and amenities, judge them by their beauty, usefulness, or indulgent qualities. Make them endearing but not overwhelming. Consider a basket of toiletries, thirsty towels, a luscious robe, and a suitcase stand as functional and fabulous additions. A phone, radio/CD

GUEST ROOM

player, and TV are modern conveniences that are always appreciated. Scented candles, fresh flowers, bottled water, fruit, and snacks add to the indulgence quotient of the space. The key to creating the ultimate guest room—soulful simplicity. Keep it restful, comforting, and reflective of your personal style.

The only gift is a portion of thyself.

Ralph Waldo Emerson

The guest room is a reflection of your hospitality. With every detail you lavish upon this space, you tell its occupants how much you care. A vase of their favorite flowers, a pot of their favorite tea, or a selection of their favorite magazines and authors are simple ways to reveal your thoughtfulness and happiness about their stay. Nothing will be more appreciated or remembered by your guests.

PAGE 118
Today, the use of twin beds in the guest room is becoming more popular. They add character, versatility, and open space to the room. The charm of this two-bed suite is derived from its minimal furnishings, simple décor, and timeless European details.

LEFT
The magic of a great guest room is often amplified by its unique design. This inviting room delights with open French doors, antique tables, and a bed angled from the corner. A stunning screen fills the corner behind the bed anchoring it to the walls.

One of the best ways to judge the appeal of your guest room is to stay in it yourself. Treat yourself to an evening "away" and indulge in all the details you have bestowed upon the room. By doing this, you will experience the luxuries and shortcomings of the space before your guests arrive. Immediately following your stay, fix the faults and relish the virtues of the space.

When detailing your guest room, remember what it is not. It is not a storage space. If you do keep things in the closets or drawers of this room, box them or hang them in garment bags to keep the hanging and folding areas open and tidy. It also is not your master bedroom. The personal details perfectly at home in your private chamber may be too personal and overwhelming for a guest room. The detail and decoration here should be tempered and impersonal. Family photos, sizable collections, and cluttered detail are not suitable. The guest's retreat refreshes the spirit and soothes the soul with its understated and relaxed ambience.

RIGHT
Equipped with soft reading light, books, fresh flowers, and an uncluttered area at which to write or read, this charming Old World writing desk makes a wonderful addition to this bedroom.

FAR RIGHT
The guest room does not need much to become a favorite for visiting friends and family. A stunning bed, luxurious linens, and a comfortable place to sit are wonderful welcoming elements; so are fresh flowers and distinctive accessories.

Good design is always evolving, shifting with our tastes, and changing with the new purposes we assign to a space. Perhaps this is no more apparent than with a child's room. Its design actually grows with the child. For example, the details that dress the room of a newborn, both decorative and practical, differ from those of a toddler's. These details continually change throughout the childhood and teenage years of the room's resident. As a child ages, the bedroom's design becomes based less on the personal tastes of the parents and more on those of the child. Clearly, adaptability and flexibility is the key to creating great children's rooms.

CHILD'S ROOM

Think back on when you were a child. Do you remember how important your bedroom was to you? In many ways, a child's room is his or her universe. It should be magical. Like a nursery rhyme, it should be filled with color, playfulness, and wonder. As the child grows, so should the room. The tastes, interests, and activities of the child should influence its fanciful design. The room becomes a world unto itself; one focused on playing, studying, and, of course, sleeping. As a child becomes a teen, the bedroom becomes a statement of individuality, a personal space somewhat off-limits to others in the home. Throughout these growing years, the two words "my room" have very special meaning. They refer to a detail-rich space filled with ever-changing design that reflects the evolving tastes and interests of the room's primary resident.

A nursery is created for both the baby and his or her caregivers. Its primary furnishings should include a crib or cradle, a piece in which to store clothing, and a table or surface for changing diapers. A comfortable chair to sit in while rocking an infant to sleep proves invaluable. Beyond these pieces, decorative detail takes over. Color, whether bright and primary or soft and soothing, fills the space. Pattern adds interest and themes emerge. Whimsical shapes, storybook characters, and murals come alive on stenciled, bordered, and papered walls. Ceilings painted with clouds and adorned with magical mobiles create interest overhead. Shelves are flush with stuffed animals and toys. The options are endless. Ideally designed, this space should be intriguing and comforting for the child as well as the parents.

PAGE 125
In this wonderfully designed nursery, no surface or furnishing goes untreated. Bold colors and patterns boost the space's striking character, while a luxurious seating area balances the more practical yet richly detailed necessities of the space.

ABOVE
Pastel colors comfort and soft lighting soothes. Light blue walls calm and cool the space, while adjustable shutters moderate its daylight. This style of window treatment is ideal for a child's room. It can remain permanent as the remainder of the space changes through the years.

LEFT
Simple white furnishings are pleasing to the eye and easy to decorate around. This nursery turns to fun-filled bedding and toys to bring color into the space.

RIGHT
This charming nursery makes good use of the corner space by placing the crib at an angle. Offering something for everybody, the room mixes the fanciful decoration on the walls and storage pieces with a more sophisticated detail on the upholstery and flooring.

ABOVE
Beautifully decorated for a girl or a visiting grand-daughter, this bedroom incorporates fine furnishings with colorfully patterned fabrics. The room's timeless detail and decoration make the space suitable for an adult guest, as well.

OPPOSITE LOWER LEFT
Bunk beds have always been a favorite for children of all ages. This room makes the most of the space by incorporating storage drawers beneath the beds and

a chest of drawers between them. The timeworn paint and ranch-hand accessories create the fun-filled ambience of a raucous bunkhouse.

OPPOSITE RIGHT
The delightful entry to this little girl's bedroom clues one in to the fanciful space within. Like a garden cottage, the room is covered with ivy trim. Lattice creates a wonderful backdrop for the antique iron bed. Sky blue ceilings and soft natural light complete the storybook look.

A child's bedroom is a reflection of his or her interests and tastes. These can change with the wink of an eye and, as they do, so should the design and décor of the space. By remaining flexible, the room can adapt to the growth of the child, with only minor growing pains of its own. An understated wood or carpeted floor can be a constant in the room, while decorative rugs can be swapped as a child ages. For the walls, paint is the easiest way to change the look and feel of a room. A vibrant primary tone may be the favorite for a school-aged child's playroom/bedroom, but a more subtle shade is normally preferred by teens. For the room's furnishings, it is best to invest in timelessly styled, quality beds and dressers that will take the room through childhood and adolescence. Leave the fads and fashion to the less expensive and easily changed accessories and accents. Built-in shelves are a wonderful place to store and display a child's toys and games. They later become home to trophies, books, and pictures of friends and family collected by teens and young adults. The key is to invest well in the permanent features of the room, and use detail to infuse the room with the whimsical tastes of the growing child.

As today's sleeping sanctuary has become multipurpose, its boundaries have expanded into an assortment of shared spaces that stretch the definition of the traditionally styled bedroom. Additionally, the same attention to detail lavished on the bedroom is repeated within these distinctive areas. Today, bedroom doors often open onto beautiful balconies and alluring patios. Evocative flooring and wall treatments of the main space flow into these outdoor areas, while shared accent colors and accessories tie the spaces together. Large closets become elaborate dressing rooms that are appointed with customized storage, skylights, and oftentimes, sumptuous seating that complements that in the suite.

OFF THE BEDROOM

Architectural alcoves and linen closets are transformed into small work areas with built-in desks and bookshelves. With the close of a door or pull of a curtain, these working areas become invisible to the relaxed nature of the bedroom. Kitchenettes and secondary laundries serve master bedrooms that are located a great distance from the home's primary cooking and laundry areas. They make the bedroom a self-sufficient home-away-from-home that indulges its owners. Of course, separate seating, lounging, and entertainment areas that are decked out in dramatic detail double the space, use, and luxury of the bedroom. They, and other uniquely styled and shared spaces, help turn an everyday bedroom into a wondrous "suite" dream.

We all find magic in different parts of our home.

Dominique Browning

PAGE 131
To tie two functionally disparate areas together, integrate decorative details from one space into the other. The distinctive floor of this vibrant bedroom extends to an enticing patio, thus merging the interior room with the exterior landscape.

OPPOSITE
Creating a personal refuge means you can be as extravagant or restrained as you like. This contemporary master suite enlists the room's architecture to house a built-in, fully functioning kitchenette and imposing metal-framed fireplace.

LEFT
A tight closet is transformed into a small working space complete with a desk, lamp, and display shelves. This wonderfully conceived feature provides a place to work and study without absorbing floor space from the main area of the bedroom.

Give your off-the-bedroom spaces the royal treatment and crown them with the same distinctive detail you bestowed upon the main area of the room. Have fun as you consider the many ways to ply them with your personal style. Try the unexpected. Hang a chandelier in a walk-in closet. Lavish an around-the-corner, outdoor bench with the same decorative pillows used on the bed. Build a wet bar in an architectural niche and team it with mirrored walls and glass shelves. Create an in-suite sitting area that rivals that in the home's main living room. Be daring and don't hesitate. After all, this is your dream bedroom and it should be everything you want it to be.

UPPER LEFT
Make the most of a bedroom's bay window by creating a built-in bench seat that is covered with plush cushions and pillows. Add an accent table and side chair, and you will have a sitting area that is sure to be a favorite on bright sunny days.

LOWER RIGHT
Extravagant moldings, a handcrafted storage island, and a crystal chandelier turn a roomy walk-in closet into a fantasy dressing room. All it takes is detail.

OPPOSITE
There is no reason your bedroom retreat should not be the most luxurious room in the home. This spacious master suite is divided into two magnificent spaces—a glamorous sleeping area and a richly appointed sitting area. Different flooring levels and half-walls define and divide the spaces while golden walls and luxurious fabrics unite them.

How boring would your bedroom be if its design were based upon the expectations of others? After all, this is your space, your private domain, and its décor should reflect your unique tastes, and personal style. It is the one place in the home where you can set your imagination free and create a room as indulgent as you like. Cover the surfaces in the treatments and colors that you love. Design your fantasy bed and dress it in luxurious cloud-like linens. Be ingenious with the furnishings you choose, and accent the space with objects you revere and treasure. Keep in mind that whatever form your dream bedroom takes, it must reflect your passions and personality to truly be your private retreat.

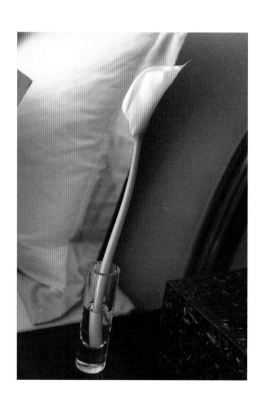

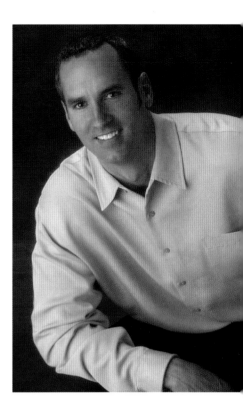

Brad Mee is a writer and author who specializes in interiors and homes. *Bedrooms: Design Is in the Details* is the fourth of a nationally renowned publication series that he has created. It follows *Design Is in the Details*, *Kitchens: Design Is in the Details*, and *Bathrooms: Design Is in the Details*, which also celebrate the power of detail in creating unique and beautifully personalized spaces. Brad is the editor of *Utah Style & Design Magazine* and divides his time between Salt Lake City, Utah, and Phoenix, Arizona.

From the Author

I would like to express my appreciation all those who made this book possible. Behind every page is the work of some incredibly talented people. To the creative interior designers, architects, builders, and manufacturers whose talents are showcased throughout the book, thank you. Your work truly defines the dream bedroom. To the extraordinary photographers who captured the essence of these beautiful rooms and brought them to light, I am indebted. My gratitude also goes to the gracious home owners who opened the doors of their bedrooms to give us a glimpse of their spectacular sanctuaries. I am especially grateful to my friends and colleagues at Chapelle, Ltd., for their continued support and encouragement. Special thanks to David Miller for his talent and generous input. I would like to recognize the talents of *Phoenix Home & Garden Magazine* editor Linda J. Barkman, and art director and photo stylist Margie Van Zee for the numerous images featured that were originally seen in that publication. My appreciation as well to *Utah Style & Design Magazine* and publishers John and Margaret Mary Shuff for their enthusiastic support. Finally, my sincerest thanks to photographer Dino Tonn for his brilliant talent and the dedication he continues to bring to the *Design Is in the Details* series.

ACKNOWLEDGMENTS

The author would like to thank the following for contributing photography to this book:

Dino Tonn Photography
5433 East Kathleen Road
Phoenix, Arizona 85254
(602) 765-0455
An attention to detail and true artistry in lighting have made Tonn one of the leading architectural photographers in the southwest. Specializing in award-winning architectural and golf-course photography, Tonn has been photographing much of the southwest's finest architecture for the past 13 years. He serves clients in the hospitality field as well as architects, interior designers, developers, and many other design-related businesses and publications. His work has been featured in regional and national publications. Tonn is a native of Arizona, and resides in Scottsdale with his wife and two children.

Christiaan Blok - Photographer
(602) 667-5577
Phoenix, Arizona
www.cblok.com
A native of the Netherlands, Blok has pursued a career in architectural and interior photography. After graduating in 1990 from the Brooks Institute of Photography in Santa Barbara, California, he settled in Phoenix, Arizona, where he is currently based. He works worldwide for magazines and book projects and shoots on a regular basis for *Traditional Home*, *Southern Accents*, and *Phoenix Home & Garden*.

Lydia Cutter - Photographer
1029 North George Mason Drive
Arlington, Virginia 22205
(703) 741-0424
A specialist in interior photography, Cutter has been serving residential and commercial clients nationally for over 21 years. In addition to her photography, she produces fine art that adorns beautiful homes and unique commercial buildings throughout the country. Her photographic work has been featured in national and regional publications. Cutter now resides in Arlington, Virginia.

Pam Singleton - Photographer
P.O. Box 783
Scottsdale, Arizona 85252
(480) 946-3246
www.azphotobook.com
www.photoexcursions.com
Singleton has been capturing images of the southwest for over 17 years, as well as photographing architecture, interiors, and landscapes. Singleton shares her love of the desert through teaching photo workshops in the Scottsdale area.

Bill Timmerman - Photographer
382 North 1st Avenue
Phoenix, Arizona 85003
(602) 420-9325
A professional photographer for 25 years, Timmerman's primary focus became architectural photography after his images of the Phoenix Central Library (architect Will Bruder) were published internationally. His ever-expanding clientele includes accomplished contemporary architects and interior designers. He has been a resident of Phoenix, Arizona, for 16 years.

Scot Zimmerman - Photographer
P.O. Box 289
261 North 400 West
Heber City, Utah 84032-0289
(800) 654-7897
zimfolks@sprynet.com
Zimmerman is an architectural photographer. During the last 20 years, his accomplishments include: photographing and producing seven books, having his photographs featured in over 48 books, regular contributions to national and regional architectural and home & garden publications, and ongoing assignments across the country. Six museums have exhibited his work nationally.

Maurice Sartirana - Photographer
Alternative Werx
Phoenix, Arizona
(602) 789-9488
altwerx@aol.com

Dawson Design Associates
4638 North 40th Street
Phoenix, Arizona 85018
(602) 955-3099
Dawson Design Associates is a full-service interior design firm bringing experience, knowledge, and innovative design to each and every design project.

David Michael Miller Associates
7034 East First Avenue
Scottsdale, Arizona 85251
(480) 425-7545
David Michael Miller Associates specializes in custom residential design and custom furniture design, from concept to completion. Miller, owner and principal, is committed to creating unique and beautiful environments for his clients. His sensitivity to organic materials, colors, and forms strongly influences his unique assemblage of art and objects. Miller's talent and projects have been recognized in interior design and home & garden magazines nationwide. His work has also been published in numerous interior design books.

Heather Ryan
H. Ryan Studio
Phoenix, Arizona
(602) 508-1770 by appt
www.hryanstudio.com

H. Ryan Studio specializes in mixing modern and antique furniture with sophisticated lines, colors, and textures to reflect one's lifestyle. Ryan, lead designer, blends her signature linens and furniture with art by David Joseph Laubenthal to create one-of-a-kind aesthetics for residential and commercial clients.

Akins/Berry Communications, Inc.
www.akinsberry.com

Founded by Rob Akins and Mark Berry, Akins/Berry Communications, Inc., is a California-based, award-winning, marketing communications company that provides a range of services which include advertising, graphic design, public relations and product launches for the home furnishings, retail, hospitality, travel, food & wine, and luxury goods markets.

Drexel Heritage
www.drexelheritage.com

Drexel Heritage offers an amazing variety of fine home furnishings, from light to dark finishes, informal to formal style categories. Drexel Heritage is one of the oldest and largest manufacturers of fine furniture in the world. The company's passion is to design and produce furniture of exceptional quality to enhance the look of your home and the way you live.

Henredon
www.henredon.com

Founded in 1945, Henredon designs and manufactures some of the finest home furnishings available. It is known by people of discriminating tastes as the best America has to offer. Henredon fine-quality home furnishings include hundreds of beautiful wood and upholstery designs for every room.

Kreiss Collection
www.kreiss.com

Kreiss Collection offers a singular blend of timeless inspiration and classic styling expressed in the finest materials, finishes, textures, fabrics, and accessories. A Kreiss room mixes geographies and influences, with a style for every taste, every mood, and every moment. Enjoy infinite possibilities for customizing your home beautifully with Kreiss.

Thibaut
www.thibautdesign.com

Established in 1886, Thibaut is the nation's oldest continuously operating wallpaper firm. Known for a fresh inspiring color palette with classic style, Thibaut offers unsurpassed quality and design in styles ranging from historic reproductions, toile, and chinoiserie to tropical and novelty patterns. With an insightful knowledge of trends and what home owners want, Thibaut consistently delivers uniquely designed collections, supported by excellent service.

CREDITS

PHOTOGRAPHY

Christiaan Blok, Phoenix, AZ 7(ctr) 11, 43, 57, 64(ll), 67, 69, 95, 99, 118–119. Photostyling–43

Lydia Cutter, Arlington, VA 5, 6(ctr)(r), 9, 25, 27–28, 41, 44–46, 56, 84(ur), 94(ur), 98(ll), 101, 107, 109(ll), 127, 130–131

Maurice Sartirana, Phoenix, AZ 77, 139(lr)

Pam Singleton, Phoenix, AZ 25, 58, 65, 70(ll)

Bill Timmerman, Phoenix, AZ 1–3, 6(l), 12, 18–21, 22(ul)(ll)(lr), 23, 35(l), 59, 63, 78, 79(ll)(ur), 92(ul)(ll), 98(ul)(lr), 103(ul), 106(ul)(ll), 133, 144

Dino Tonn, Scottsdale, AZ cover, 7(r), 15–16, 17(ul)(ll), 29, 31, 33–34, 35(r), 38–39, 47, 49–50, 54(ul)(lr), 55, 60–62, 71–72, 75–76, 80(ll), 81, 83, 84(lr), 85, 86(r), 87(r), 89, 93, 97, 100(ul)(lr), 102, 103(ll), 108, 112, 115–116, 120, 122–125; 128, 134(lr), 135

Margie Van Zee (photostylist) ph:(602) 695-2054, Phoenix, AZ 7(ctr), 11, 29, 34, 38, 39, 50, 57, 64(ll), 67, 69, 71, 76, 81, 86, 87, 95, 97, 99, 100(ul)(lr), 108, 116, 118–119, 122–123, 135

Scot Zimmerman, Heber City, UT 53, 64(ur), 111, 126(ll)(ur), 129(ll)(r), 132

INTERIOR DESIGNERS

Anita Lang Mueller, Interior Motives, Fountain Hills, AZ 39

Ann Bitters 95

Anne Gale, Wiseman & Gale Interiors, Scottsdale, AZ 134(lr)

Bess Jones Interiors, Scottsdale, AZ 54(ul), 80(ll), 135

Betsy Bradley, Salt Lake City, UT 53

Billi Springer Interior Design, Scottsdale, AZ 86(r)

Bouton/Foley Interiors, Paradise Valley, AZ 49

Carlyn & Company Interior Design, Great Falls, VA 84(ur)

Carol Minchew ASID, Carol Minchew Interiors, Scottsdale, AZ 50

Chistopher Coffin, Wiseman & Gale Interiors, Scottsdale, AZ 116

David Michael Miller, David Michael Miller Associates, Scottsdale, AZ cover, 1–3, 6(l), 12–13, 15, 18–21, 22(ul)(ll)(lr), 23, 28, 35(l), 47, 59, 63, 78, 79(ll)(ur), 89, 92(ul)(ll), 96, 98(ul)(lr), 102–103, 106(ul)(ll), 133, 144

David Mitchell Interior Design, Washington, D.C. 44–45, 94(ur), 98(ll), 107, 109(ll)

Dawson Design Associates, Maria Dawson, Phoenix, AZ 14, 73(l)(ctr)

Debra Anderson, Salt Lake City, UT 132

Debra May Himes Interior Design & Assoc., Mesa, AZ 55

Donna Vallone, Vallone Design, Inc., Scottsdale, AZ 71, 85

European Design, Scottsdale, AZ 93

Fannin Interiors, Phoenix, AZ 9

Friedman & Shields, Scottsdale, AZ 17(ul)(ll), 62, 83

Gloria Wedlake, Valerianne of Scottsdale, Scottsdale, AZ 75

Heather Ryan, H. Ryan Studio, Phoenix, AZ 77, 139(lr)

Jamie Herzlinger Interiors, Phoenix, AZ 127–128

Jennifer Hoage, Christalie Interiors, Phoenix, AZ 81

John Told, Midway, UT 64(ur)

Kim Anderson, Vallone Design Inc., Scottsdale, AZ 124–125

Lawrence Lake, Inter Plan Design Group, Scottsdale, AZ 65

Lisa Walker, ASID, Walker Design Group, Scottsdale, AZ 16

Luis Corona and Michael Barron, Casa del Encanto, Scottsdale, AZ 27, 29, 108

Marcie Saban Pound Interiors, Scottsdale, AZ 38

Marsha Amato, Interior Designations, Scottsdale, AZ 87(r), 97, 122

KEY

(l) = left

(r) = right

(u) = upper

(l) = lower

(ctr) = center

140

Marsha Graber, Graber Design, Ltd., Scottsdale, AZ 54(lr)

Mary Ellen Klein, MPK Holdings Design Team 111

Montie Simmons, AZ 58

Paula Berg, Paula Berg Design Associates, Scottsdale, AZ, Park City, UT 5, 6(ctr)(r), 25, 41, 46, 76, 101, 130–131

Peter Magee, Scottsdale, AZ 7(r), 33

Sharon Fekuda, Designs, Salt Lake City, UT 126(ll)(ur), 129(r)

Shelly Duane, Revelations Interiors 7(ctr), 99

Taulbee Design Group, Joe Taulbee 67

Tamm Jasper Interiors, Scottsdale, AZ 60, 112

Tennen Studio 35(r)

Teresa DeLellis Design Assoc., Carefree, AZ 56, 61, 70(ll)

Teri Mulmed, Do Daz, Inc., Design Firm, Scottsdale, AZ 84(lr), 115

Vickee Banta, Emerald Design, Sunriver, OR 72

William Hargrave Interior Designer, Flagstaff, AZ 100(lr)

ARCHITECTS

Abramson Teiger Architects, Culver City, CA 3(l)(r), 20, 21(ur)(lr), 23, 78, 79(ur)

Alan Tafoya Architect, Carefree, AZ 86(r)

Bing Hu, H & S Enterprises, Scottsdale, AZ 15

Bob Easton, Santa Barbara, CA 2

Bokal & Sneed Architects, Del Mar, CA 3(ctr), 6(l), 18–19, 22(ul)(lr), 79(ll), 92(ul)

Ethan Wessel & Sarah Swartz Wessel of Tennen Studio 35(r)

H & S International, Scottsdale, AZ cover, 31, 47, 89, 106(ll)

Jan Mittlestadt, Phoenix, AZ 100(ul)

John DeGray, Park City, UT 129(ll)

Peter M. Magee 7(r), 33

Rick Daugherty Architect, Scottsdale, AZ 123

RJ Bacon Co., Phoenix; AZ 61

Urban Design Associates; Scottsdale, AZ 54(ul), 72

ART

David Laubenthal, Portland, OR 77

BUILDERS

DeLellis Construction; Carefree, AZ 61

Gill Builders Company 55

Magee Custom Homes, LLC 7(r), 33

Phoenix Smith & Co., Inc. 62, 83

RS Homes; Scottsdale, AZ 54(ul)

Salcito Custom Homes; Scottsdale, AZ 60, 80(ll), 84(lr), 112, 135

Tennen Construction 35(r)

Wall St. West Development; Scottsdale, AZ 31

CABINET DESIGN

Armoire-Ellis Woods 61

European Design Custom Cabinet; Scottsdale, AZ Alan Rosenthal 93

PRODUCTS

Drexel Heritage 24, 26, 40(ll), 48(ul)(ll), 82, 90, 94(ul), 104, 143

Henredon 48(lr), 70(ul), 73(r), 109(u)

Kreiss Collection 36–37, 40(ul), 80(ul), 91, 94(lr), 105, 114, 136–137, 142

Thibaut 22(ur), 94(ll), 134

PHOTODISKS

Photodisc, Inc., Images (©1999, 2001) 30, 52, 74, 79(lr), 117(ll)(r), 121, 139(ur)

Every effort has been made to credit all contributors. We apologize in advance for any unintentional omission and would be pleased to insert the appropriate acknowledgment in any subsequent editions.

If you can't get to sleep, try lying on the other end of the bed—
you might drop off.

Anonymous

142